How Do Boats Float?

by Nairobi Toller

PEARSON
Scott
Foresman

What You Already Know

Everything you see, smell, or touch is matter. Many things you cannot see, smell, or touch are matter too. Matter is anything that takes up space and has mass. You can observe the properties of matter.

Matter comes in three forms: solid, liquid, and gas. Solid matter particles are packed tightly together. Liquid matter particles are loosely connected. Gaseous matter particles are not connected. When gas is put into a closed space, it expands, pushing against the sides of the container. This pushing is called pressure.

Some kinds of matter are made up of only one type of particle. This single type of matter is called an element. Elements are made up of even smaller particles called atoms. There are more than one hundred different elements. Scientists organize the elements in a periodic table, or chart of elements.

Properties of matter can be measured. Mass is the amount of matter an object has. It can be measured with a balance.

Volume is the amount of space an object takes up. Volume is most often measured in liters.

Density is a property that measures the amount of matter in a certain amount of space. Two objects of the same volume can have different densities because of their mass.

Buoyancy is a property of matter that measures how well an object floats. Objects more dense than water sink. Objects less dense than water float.

In this book you will learn more about density, buoyancy, and other properties of matter in water. These are all things that engineers must think about in order to build ships that float.

Floating and Sinking

Have you ever wondered how huge ships are able to float? Even cargo ships loaded down with heavy goods float. Buoyancy and density make floating possible. Engineers who build ships must think about how to make heavy things, such as cargo ships, have a low enough density to float in water.

Most ships are made with lots of metal screws. But if you throw a metal screw into water, it will sink. At first you may think this is because the screw is heavy. But weight alone does not make it sink. The screw sinks because of its density. The density of most metal is greater than the density of water.

Most ships are made of metal too. It does not seem as though ships should float. All that metal and all those screws sink on their own. How do the engineers combine them so a ship can float?

Screws sink because they have a greater density than water.

This huge cargo ship floats because it has a lot of buoyancy.

Matter and Density

The secret to making objects float is density. Density is the amount of mass an object has in a certain volume. One liter of water has a mass of 1 kilogram (kg). The same volume of steel has a mass of nearly 8 kg. The mass of a one-liter volume of balsa wood is just $\frac{1}{5}$ kg.

A solid object will float on the surface of a liquid if it has a lower density than the liquid. Balsa wood is less dense than water. So balsa wood floats on water. Steel is denser than water. It sinks in water.

cooking oil

water

syrup

Liquids of different densities separate into layers when poured into the same glass.

Which matter has the lowest density? Which has the greatest?

A cork floats on oil.

A plastic block sinks in oil but floats on water.

A grape sinks in oil and water but floats on syrup.

Not all liquids have the same density. Some liquids have more mass and a higher density than others. Syrup is more dense than water. Water is more dense than oil. Liquids of different densities will separate into layers when poured into the same container. The lower-density liquids float on top. The higher-density liquids sink to the bottom.

Place solid objects in the same container. Then you can see how dense they are in comparison with the other objects and liquids. The more dense objects will sink lower in the container in the same way more dense liquids sink lower.

Forces in Water

What happens when you place an object into water? It pushes aside, or displaces, some of the water. The volume of water displaced equals the volume of the object. As a stone sinks in water, it pushes aside an amount of water equal to its own volume. Even floating objects displace an amount of water equal to their volume.

Objects feel lighter as you lower them into water. This is because the water pushes against them with an upward force. Objects sink until this force balances their weight. But some objects sink to the bottom. This is because they are denser than water. The upward force of the water is not strong enough to balance the object's weight.

This peach has displaced only the amount of water equal to its weight. The peach is buoyant because the upward force of the water balances its weight.

The upward force of the water makes a cargo ship buoyant.

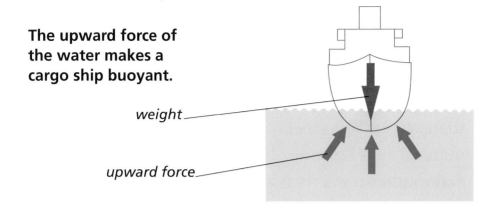

weight

upward force

Upward force creates buoyancy. Buoyancy partly supports the object. The amount of upward force depends on the amount of water pushed aside by the object. The more water something displaces, the greater the upward force on it. If the upward force is equal to the weight of the object, the object floats.

Archimedes

The Greek scientist Archimedes discovered that objects get an upward force from displaced water. He noticed this when he took a bath.

Shape and Volume

You already know that steel is more dense than water. But steel can be shaped in a way that increases its volume. The volume of an object can increase, yet its mass can stay the same. That decreases the object's density.

The body, or hull, of a ship is designed with a huge open space in the front and bottom. The ship's hull takes up a lot of space but weighs very little for its size. It contains a large volume of air, which lowers the density of the ship. The density is now less than water, so the ship can float!

The huge, hollow hull on this cargo ship allows it to float.

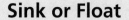

Sink or Float

A piece of clay shaped into a ball will sink. But the same piece of clay shaped like a ship's hull will float. It has enough volume inside to displace enough water to carry a cargo of marbles too.

A clay ball and marbles sink.

Boat-shaped clay floats and holds marbles.

The large volume of the hull means the ship displaces a lot of water. All the displaced water creates a powerful upward force that supports the ship.

If the same amount of steel used to build a ship were shaped differently, would it float? A solid block of steel is much more dense than water. If it were put into water, it would sink.

Controlling Buoyancy

The density of submarines, human divers, and fish can be adjusted to control buoyancy.

A ship's hull is full of air. This helps it float. Submarines can float or sink. They use special tanks to do this. These tanks can be filled with water or air. When the tanks are full of water, the submarine becomes more dense than water. It sinks. When water is released from the tanks, the submarine becomes less dense, Then it floats.

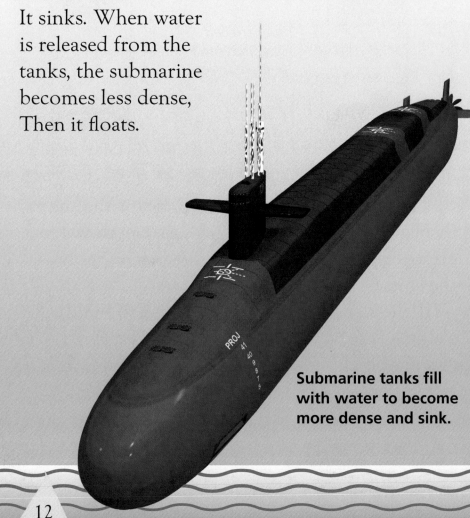

Submarine tanks fill with water to become more dense and sink.

People have air and organs in their bodies that make them less dense than water. This allows them to float. Divers must wear belts with weights on them to increase their density. Then they are able to sink below the surface.

Most fish are able to adjust their own buoyancy. They can do this using an organ called a swim bladder. When a fish swims deep, water pressure pushes gas out of the bladder. The fish becomes more dense and sinks. To rise to the surface, gas fills the bladder. This makes the fish less dense so it can float.

Divers use weighted belts so they can control their buoyancy.

Water Pressure

Water presses down on objects. This pressing force, or pressure, becomes stronger in deeper water.

You can experiment with water pressure using a plastic tube and water. Put three holes in the tube. Put one at the bottom, one in the middle, and one at the top. Fill the tube with water. Watch to see how far the water shoots out of each hole. The water from the bottom hole shoots out the farthest. That is where the water pressure is greatest. The water pressure is weaker near the top, so the water does not shoot out as far.

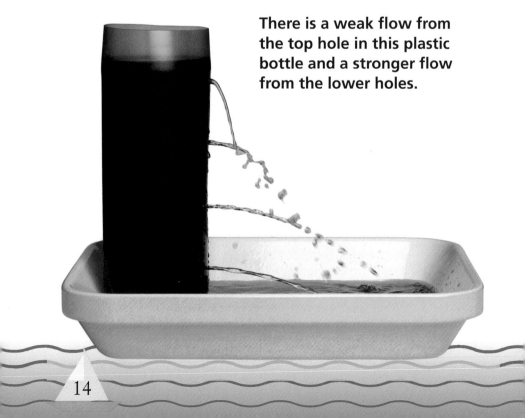

There is a weak flow from the top hole in this plastic bottle and a stronger flow from the lower holes.

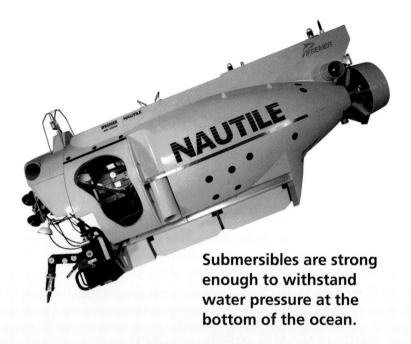

Submersibles are strong enough to withstand water pressure at the bottom of the ocean.

You can feel water pressure in your ears when you swim. People cannot swim very deep underwater. The pressure is too strong. We use submarines to travel in deep water. They are strong enough to handle the water pressure.

Yet not even a submarine is strong enough to withstand the pressure at the bottom of the ocean. Only small, very strong machines called submersibles can withstand the pressure.

Maybe someday people will be able to travel to the bottom of the ocean safely. For now, we must learn more about ways that make boats float. Density, volume, buoyancy, and water pressure help engineers build ships that can float.

Glossary

balsa wood   strong and light type of wood

cargo ship   a ship that carries goods from place to place

displace   to move from its usual place

hull   body or frame of a ship

steel   strong and hard metal made of iron mixed with carbon

swim bladder   an organ in a fish that helps it control its own density by taking in or releasing gas

withstand   to stand up to something